WELCOME TO MY COUNTRY

Welcome to
POLAND

FRANKLIN WATTS
LONDON · SYDNEY

This edition first published in 2005 by
Franklin Watts
96 Leonard Street
London EC2A 4XD

Franklin Watts Australia
45-51 Huntley Street
Alexandria NSW 2015

This edition is published for sale only in the United Kingdom & Eire.

© Marshall Cavendish International (Asia) Pte Ltd 2005
Originated and designed by Times Editions–Marshall Cavendish
an imprint of Marshall Cavendish International (Asia) Pte Ltd
A member of the Times Publishing Group
Times Centre, 1 New Industrial Road
Singapore 536196

Written by: Umaima Mulla-Feroze & Paul Grajnert
Editor: Melvin Neo
Designer: Geoslyn Lim
Picture researcher: Susan Jane Manuel

A CIP catalogue record for this book
is available from the British Library.

ISBN 0 7496 6020 1

Printed in Singapore

PICTURE CREDITS
Allsport/Stu Forster: 36
ANA Press Agency: 7 (top), 27 (top)
Art Directors & TRIP Photographic Library:
    17, 19, 22, 25, 45
Camera Press Ltd.: 7 (bottom), 8 (bottom),
    16 (both), 18, 24, 26 (bottom), 28 (bottom),
    33, 34 (both), 40 (top)
Sue Cunningham Photographic: 1, 41 (bottom)
Embassy of the Republic of Poland: 44
Focus Team – Italy: 3 (centre), 3 (bottom),
    21 (both), 23 (bottom), 30 (both), 31, 35,
    37, 40 (bottom), 43
Getty Images/Hulton Archive: 10 (both),
    11 (both), 13 (bottom), 15 (top), 29 (both)
Bridget Gubbins: 4, 9 (both), 23 (top)
PAI Fotografia: 8 (top), 12, 13 (top), 28 (top)
Chip & Rosa Maria Petersen: 2, 32 (top), 39
Reuters/Hulton Archive: 15 (bottom)
Topham Picturepoint: cover, 14 (both),
    20 (bottom), 27 (bottom), 32 (bottom),
    38, 41 (top)
Travel Ink: 3 (top), 5, 6, 20 (top), 26 (top)

Digital Scanning by Superskill Graphics Pte Ltd

Contents

Words that appear in the glossary are printed in **boldface** type the first time they occur in the text.

Welcome to Poland!

The Republic of Poland is one of the most populated countries in Central Europe. Ruled by **communists** from 1944 to 1989, Poland today has a **democratic** government, with rapid social and economic growth. Let's learn about Poland and its people.

Opposite: A Polish family from Zulawka Sztumska, a village east of Gdansk, has gathered for a picture outside their home.

Below:
The Zachęta Gallery in Warsaw has many important pieces of Polish art.

The Flag of Poland

Poland's national flag was officially adopted in 1919. It is white on top and red on the bottom. White represents peace. Red symbolises the blood of Polish **patriots** who died in their nation's struggle for peace.

The Land

Poland covers an area of 312,685 kilometres square. It is surrounded by the Baltic Sea and the countries of Russia and Lithuania to the north, Belarus and Ukraine to the east, Slovakia and the Czech Republic to the south and Germany to the west. Warsaw is the largest city and the country's capital.

Below: The town of Zakopane lies at the foot of the High Tatra Mountains, the highest range in the Carpathian Mountains.

Left: Poland has 3,812 kilometres of **navigable** rivers and canals and more than 9,000 lakes. Most of the lakes are located in the north-eastern and western regions.

Most of Poland is flat. Its northern and central regions form a vast, fertile plain. Mountains in the south and the south-west belong to the Carpathian range and the Sudeten range. Mount Rysy, Poland's highest peak, is in the Carpathian's High Tatra Mountains.

Two important **waterways** crossing Poland's central plain are the Vistula, or Wisla, River and the Oder, or Odra, River. Both rivers flow north to the Baltic Sea, and both provide water and transportation routes for large cities.

Below: Pollution is a big problem in Poland's many rivers and lakes.

Climate

Poland's **moderate** climate has six seasons. Early spring weather, from March to May, varies from wintry to mild. Late spring, in May and June, is sunny. A warm, rainy summer, with an average temperature of about 22° Celsius, starts in July. Autumn in September is warm, then turns cool and damp in October. December brings a snowy winter.

Above: Skiing is a popular winter activity in Poland.

Below: Southern Poland has a lot of snow in winter.

Plants and Animals

Forests of beech, fir, spruce and pine in the southern mountains, along with the wetlands of the north-east, are the only major areas of Poland that remain undisturbed by human inhabitants.

Wolves and brown bears live in the mountain areas. Elk, deer and wild sheep roam freely in the north-eastern region. Birds found in Poland include Pomeranian eagles, tawny owls and black storks. Salmon, trout and carp are some of the fish in Poland's rivers.

Above: Bialowieza National Park, near Bialystok, has a large herd of rare European bison.

Below: This woman is using special equipment to track wolves in eastern Poland.

History

From about A.D.100, a group of Slavs known as the Polanie settled on the central plains of Poland. They later united with other Slavs to form the kingdom of Poland. King Mieszko I, of the Piast **dynasty**, who reigned from about 963 to 992, is considered the founder of the Polish state. Under the Piast dynasty (966–1382), Poland grew to be a major European power.

Below:
Mieszko I (*left*) and Wladyslaw II Jagiello (*right*), of the Jagiellon dynasty, were important Polish kings who ruled during the Middle Ages.

Kazimierz III (r. 1333–1370) was another famous Piast king. He made laws, developed trade and allowed **persecuted** Jews to settle in Poland.

In 1386, Piast queen Jadwiga married the grand duke of Lithuania, Wladyslaw II Jagiello. Over two centuries, Jagiellon kings continued to increase Polish land. When that dynasty ended, the Sejm, a group of powerful nobles, elected Poland's kings until 1795.

The Fall and Rise of Poland

Weak leadership, corruption and constant fighting within the country led neighbouring Russia, Prussia, the former kingdom of Germany, and Austria to **annex** Poland's land. In 1772, Poland lost one-fourth of its territory to these countries.

Believing that political **reform** was the only way to free their country from foreign rule, the Sejm passed the Constitution of 3 May 1791. Russia, Prussia and Austria saw this constitution as a threat. In 1793, Russian and Prussian

Left: *Battle at Grunwald* is an eighteenth-century painting showing Polish soldiers attacking German warriors in 1410.

Left: In 1939, Nazi troops invading Poland set up road blocks in the country.

troops invaded Poland and took more of its land. The Polish fought against these forces but were defeated in 1795.

With help from Britain, France and the United States of America, Poland regained its independence, but not until after World War I (1914–1918). For the unstable Polish nation, however, independence was short-lived. World War II (1939–1945) started when Nazi Germany and the Soviet Union invaded Poland and took control of the country. After the war, Poland remained under Soviet communist rule for 44 years.

Below: During World War II, the Nazis put to death millions of Polish Jews at **concentration camps** such as Auschwitz.

The Solidarity Movement

In 1980, factory workers throughout Poland went on strike, demanding democracy and more human rights. This Solidarity Movement, led by an electrician named Lech Walesa (1943–), succeeded. In 1989, in the nation's first open elections, Poles voted for a non-communist government.

Below (*left*): This street in Warsaw is an example of the destruction that occurred during World War II.

Below (*right*): The same street in 1955 shows how Warsaw was rebuilt after the war.

Maria Konopnicka (1842–1910)

Throughout her life, Polish poet and novelist Maria Konopnicka played an active role in organisations that protested the persecution of Poles by the Russians and the Prussians.

Tadeusz Mazowiecki (1927–)

An important anti-communist figure in the 1980s, lawyer and journalist Tadeusz Mazowiecki was elected as Poland's first non-communist leader after the war. As editor of the official publication of the Solidarnosc trade union, Mazowiecki played a major role in the Solidarity Movement.

Tadeusz Mazowiecki

Adam Malysz (1978–)

One of the world's top ski-jumpers, Adam Malysz has made this sport popular both in Poland and abroad. At the 2001 World Cup competition in Oslo, Norway, Malysz jumped a near-record 124 metres.

Adam Malysz

Government and the Economy

Poland is a **constitutional republic**. In 1997, the country adopted a new constitution that guarantees the rights of the Polish people and sets up a national government. The president, who is elected by the people, and the prime minister, appointed by the president, lead the government. Laws are passed by a parliament with two chambers, the Senate and the Sejm.

Above: A special gallery in Poland's parliament allows members of the general public to view proceedings.

16

Parliament's 100 senators and the 460 deputies of the Sejm, or House of Representatives, are elected by the people, all for four-year terms. In Poland's justice system, the president appoints Supreme Court judges, and the Sejm selects the judges who serve on the Constitutional Tribunal.

Poland has three different levels of local government: village or small town, county and provincial.

Above: The Polish military includes an army, a navy, an air force and an air defence force. All male citizens who are twenty-seven years and older must have military training and must serve in Poland's military for at least one year.

Opposite: The Presidential Palace in Warsaw was built in the 1600s.

The Economy

When communism ended in Poland, the country's economy changed from state-controlled to a free market. More than 70 per cent of all Polish goods and services today are provided by private companies. About 27 per cent of the total workforce have agricultural jobs. Another 22 per cent are employed in the manufacturing, construction and mining industries. The rest work in service jobs, such as transportation.

Above: Among the countries in Eastern Europe, Poland has one of the strongest economies, and new laws have made setting up businesses easier.

Natural Resources

Poland's fertile agricultural land is its main natural resource. More than half of the land is **cultivated**. Crops include potatoes, fruits and leafy vegetables. Forests, which cover almost 30 per cent of the country, are valuable resources for Poland's important timber and paper industries. Poland also has rich coal and metal deposits for mining and is a world leader in silver production.

Below: Many old factories that were built when Poland was a communist country are now worthless and are being torn down.

People and Lifestyle

About 97 per cent of Poland's more than 38 million people are Polish. Among the remaining 3 per cent are Germans, Ukrainians, Lithuanians, Slovaks, Belorussians and Romany Gypsies. Before World War II, over three million Jews lived in Poland, but after their brutal treatment by the Nazis, only a small group remains.

Above: Romany Gypsies are one of the **ethnic** minorities living in Poland. The largest **minority group** is German.

Left: Weddings in Poland can be as simple as getting a licence from a government office or as elaborate as an all-night party with live music and plenty of food. These newly-weds were married in traditional clothing.

Opposite: Polish families, especially those with young children, spend a lot of time together.

Under Poland's constitution, all citizens have equal rights, so minority groups can keep their own cultures and teach their native languages to their children. Some minorities even have representatives in the Sejm.

Family Life

Polish families are close-knit. Parents and grandparents often live with their children and grandchildren. As adults, most Poles do not move very far from the places where they were born.

Below: This family from the southern city of Zakopane is sharing a meal. In Poland, most leisure activities involve the whole family.

Women in Poland

In communist Poland, women were considered equal to men and were represented in Parliament, although few had active roles in politics. In democratic Poland, the traditional women's roles of homemakers and mothers are changing, and Polish women have set up organisations that discuss women's issues.

Above: Dressed in colourful ethnic clothing for a local festival in Wroclaw, these women look very traditional, but since the fall of communism in 1989, women's roles in Poland have changed.

City and Rural Life

Poles are typically gracious and well mannered, addressing strangers as *pan*, or "sir", and *pani*, or "madam". The lifestyle of city dwellers is very different from Poles living in rural areas. People in Poland's modern cities are generally better educated and have more money. Most people living in rural Poland are poor, less educated and old-fashioned in their ways. They do not trust the changes that have been taking place in Polish society.

Above: In some of Poland's rural areas, people still live in cottages with **thatch** roofs.

Below: Most Polish farms today have modern machinery but some farmers still use horses to plough the fields.

Education

Every child in Poland between the ages of 6 and 17 must go to school. The Ministry of National Education runs most of the country's schools. A few are privately owned.

After seven years of primary school, students must pass an examination to enter a *gymnasium*, or lower secondary school. Another examination, taken after three years, qualifies students for

Below: Some of Poland's primary and secondary schools are run by the Catholic Church.

24

three years of upper secondary school at a *lyceum*. Those who pass final exams can then apply to a university. Students can also prepare to enter the workforce by attending **vocational** or technical schools for two to four years after the gymnasium.

Poland has many technical colleges and universities. Founded in 1364, the Jagiellonian University of Kraków is one of the oldest universities in Europe.

Above:
A performance by a student choir is part of the ceremony for this university graduation.

Religion

Roman Catholicism is Poland's main religion. When King Mieszko I converted to Roman Catholicism in A.D. 966, Poland became recognised as a nation by western Europe and the Holy Roman Empire. Approximately 95 per cent of Poles are Roman Catholics. The rest belong to the Eastern Orthodox, Protestant or other faiths. For many modern Poles, however, practising their religion has become less important than in the past.

Above: This sixteenth-century building in Warsaw is the Carmelite Church of the Nativity.

Below: Pope John Paul II is the first Polish leader of the Catholic Church.

Polish Jews

Although Poland has always claimed to have a policy of **religious tolerance**, Polish Jews were often forced to live in **ghettos**. During World War II, some Polish Catholics showed little concern for the thousands of Jews being killed by the Nazis. In Jedwabne, Catholic Poles even killed their Jewish neighbours. Approximately 20,000 Jews still live in Poland today.

Above: Only about 75 per cent of the Catholics in Poland practice their faith.

Below: Orthodox Christians attend a church service in Kraków.

Language

Almost all people in Poland speak Polish, the country's official language. The Polish language belongs to the western Slavic language group and uses the Roman, or Latin, alphabet.

    The Polish alphabet has 32 letters. Special accent marks on some letters determine how they sound. The sound of *ó*, for example, is "OOH." Putting certain letters together creates other sounds, such as *sz* for "SH."

Above: Many old Polish manuscripts and books can be found outside Poland, some at the Library of Congress in Washington, D.C.

Left: These posters are promoting the election of Tadeusz Mazowiecki, who was Poland's first non-communist prime minister.

Literature

Pan Tadeusz, a poem written by Adam Mickiewicz in 1834, is one of Poland's most famous literary works. Its story reflects the hope for Poland's liberation during the Napoleonic wars. The well-known novel *Quo Vadis?* was written by Henryk Sienkiewicz, who won the Nobel Prize for Literature in 1905. In 1996, Wislawa Szymborska became the first Polish woman, and only the ninth woman ever, to earn this award.

Above:
Joseph Conrad (*left*), author of *Lord Jim* (1900) and *Heart of Darkness* (1902), was Polish, but he always wrote in English. Because of strict communist controls on what writers could say and not say, Jerzy Kosinski (*right*) and other Polish authors chose to leave the country and write in **exile**.

Arts

Folk art has been popular in Poland for a long time. It is an interesting hobby as well as a means of preserving Polish history. *Wycinanki* is a form of folk art in which dyed paper is cut or torn into designs. For the most elaborate designs, layers of paper are glued together. Weaving is an ancient folk art. Traditional materials such as flax and wool are used to make clothing, blankets and other everyday items.

Above: Carving decorative wooden plates and statues is one of many forms of folk art in Poland.

Left: Wood sculptures like these, which were made in Zakopane, are often on display in Polish homes.

Making **Nativity** scenes, or *szopka*, out of paper, cardboard, beads, sequins and coloured foil is a Christmas tradition in Kraków.

Folk Dancing

Folk dancing in Poland brings people together and keeps traditions alive. Polish folk dances include the *mazur* and the *kujawiak*.

Above:
Dance troupes help preserve Poland's folk dance tradition. These dancers are performing in traditional costumes at Kraków Square.

Polish Classical Music

Frédéric Chopin was Poland's most famous classical music **composer**. He used Polish folk melodies in his works and is known especially for his more than two hundred pieces of piano music.

Stanislaw Moniuszko and Henryk Wieniawski are also well-known Polish composers of the nineteenth century. Modern composers include Henryk Gorecki and Krzysztof Penderecki.

Jazz and Popular Music

After World War II, American jazz became very popular in Poland, even though it was banned by the country's communist government. Polish jazz musicians include Michal Urbaniak, a jazz violinist and composer, and Adam Makowicz, a jazz pianist.

Polish musicians play many styles of music that are popular in the United States and Western Europe, including rap, hip-hop, rock 'n' roll and country.

Below: Along with American music and movies, Poland's young people seem to like American clothing. This young Pole is looking at a T-shirt that has a picture of American actress Marilyn Monroe on it.

Leisure

Summer is vacation time in Poland. Although some younger Poles like to travel around Europe and to other parts of the world, most Polish people stay within their own country. Beach resorts on the Baltic coast are popular vacation spots, and the Mazury Lakes region attracts campers and fishing enthusiasts. Rides along the canals that connect the many lakes offer spectacular views.

Above: In Gdansk, tourists can ride a barge down a canal.

Polish families spend most of their leisure time together. Favourite outdoor activities include camping, sailing and windsurfing. Popular weekend activities include mushroom picking in country forests and picnicking in city parks.

Some city dwellers own small plots of land in the country where they have vegetable gardens. Many owners build a hut on the plot so they can spend the night when they visit their land.

Above: The High Tatra Mountains offer hikers many beautiful, scenic views. Hiking in the mountains of southern Poland is a favourite summer activity. In winter, Poles visit mountain resorts for skiing and snowboarding.

Opposite: Poles flock to beaches on the Baltic coast to swim and sunbathe.

35

Sports

Football is Poland's most popular sport. While Poles of all ages enjoy it, young Poles will play anywhere they can find enough room for a football pitch. The most devoted football fans, called *kibic*, are interested only in football news, scores and players.

Poland has been a member of the Fédération Internationale de Football Association (FIFA) since 1923, and organised football in Poland dates back to 1919. Today, the country has four levels of professional teams. The First League, or highest level, has sixteen teams. First League players represent Poland in World Cup competition.

Basketball is another popular team sport in Poland. The country's top league has fifteen teams. Polish fans will even watch National Basketball Association (NBA) games from the United States on cable television.

Below: Chess is a favourite pastime for many Poles, and bridge is a popular card game.

Festivals

Many holidays in Poland are religious festivals. Christmas Eve, or *Wigilia*, is probably the most important festival. Families enjoy a special meal together and exchange gifts. Then they attend a midnight mass called *Pasterka*, or Shepherd's Mass, in honour of the shepherds at the birth of Jesus Christ. In pre-Christian times, this day celebrated the end of the harvest season and the beginning of winter.

Below: Every year on Good Friday, the people of Kalwaria Zebrzydowska re-enact the journey of Jesus Christ to Calvary, where he was crucified.

Easter is another important religious holiday in Poland. Preparations begin on Ash Wednesday. Pussy willow twigs are cut to be blessed in church for Palm Sunday, and children decorate eggs. On Easter morning, families go to church, then return home for a feast. Before eating, they break blessed eggs and share good wishes. The next day is for fun. Young Poles celebrate by throwing buckets of water over each other.

Above:
The traditional clothing worn for Polish festivals is both elaborate and colourful.

Food

Poles typically eat three meals a day, breakfast, lunch and dinner, as well as an evening snack. Dinner, or *obiadd*, is the most important meal. It is served between 3pm and 6pm, when everyone is home from work or school. Dinner usually includes soup, a main dish of meat and vegetables, dessert and tea or coffee.

Above: Poles enjoy over one hundred kinds of sausages.
Below: Fried cheese is a Polish **delicacy**.

Left: Meat roasted outdoors is popular at feasts in towns and villages in the Sudeten Mountains.

Traditional Foods

Poland is famous for pork products such as pork chops and *kielbasa*, or sausages. Other traditional Polish foods include rye breads, sauerkraut and *pierogi*, which are dumplings, usually filled with meat, cabbage, cheese or mushrooms. *Bigos* is a thick stew of cabbage and spiced meats. Poles also enjoy soups. *Chlodnik*, a cold beetroot soup, is a summer favourite.

Below: Cookies and other sweets are an important part of any Polish feast. *Nalesniki* is a traditional Polish pancake.

41

Provinces

1 Zachodniopomorskie	**5** Lubuskie	**9** Lubelskie	**13** Swietokrzyskie
2 Pomorskie	**6** Wielkopolskie	**10** Dolnoslaskie	**14** Slaskie
3 Warminsko-Mazurskie	**7** Kujawsko-Pomorskie	**11** Opolskie	**15** Malopolskie
4 Podlaskie	**8** Mazowieckie	**12** Lodzkie	**16** Podkarpackie

Above: Once the capital city of Poland, Kraków still attracts many tourists.

Auschwitz
    Concentration
    Camp C4

Baltic Sea A1–C1
Belarus D1–D3
Bialowieza National
    Park D2
Bialystok D2

Carpathian
    Mountains
    C4–D4
Czech Republic
    A3–B4

Gdansk B1
Germany A1–A3

High Tatra
    Mountains C4

Jedwabne D2

Kalwaria
    Zebrzydowska
    C4
Kraków C4

Lithuania C1–D1
Lódz C3

Mazury Lakes
    Region C1–C2
Mount Rysy C4

Oder River
    A2–B4

Russia C1–D1

Slovakia B4–D4
Sudeten Mountains
    A3–B4

Ukraine D3–D4

Vistula River
    B1–C4

Warsaw C2
Wroclaw B3

Zakopane C4
Zulawka
    Sztumska C1

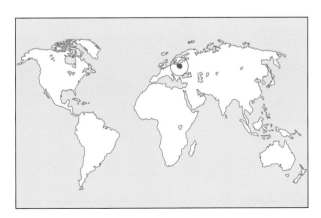

Quick Facts

Official Name Republic of Poland

Capital Warsaw

Official Language Polish

Population 38,626,349 (July 2004 estimate)

Land Area 312,685 square kilometres

Highest Point Mount Rysy 2,499 metres

Border Countries Belarus, Czech Republic, Germany, Lithuania, Russia, Slovakia, Ukraine

Mountain Ranges Carpathian Mountains, Sudeten Mountains

Major Cities Warsaw, Lódz, Kraków

Major Rivers Vistula, Oder

Major Religions Roman Catholicism, Eastern Orthodox, Protestantism

Important Holidays Easter (March/April)

Constitution Day (May 3)

Independence Day (November 11)

Christmas Day (December 25)

Currency Zloty (6.79 PLZ = £1 in July 2004)

Opposite: Peanuts are one of Poland's many agricultural products.

Glossary

annex: take possession of a country or territory to increase the size or power of another country or territory.

communists: people that belong to a political system in which the government owns and controls all goods and resources.

composer: a person who writes music.

concentration camps: fenced, guarded areas where people are held prisoner, usually for political reasons.

constitutional republic: a nation or state that is governed by elected officials according to the principles of a written constitution.

cultivated: used for growing crops.

delicacy: an uncommon food that is considered a luxury.

democratic: related to a political system of self-rule through elected representatives.

dynasty: a family of rulers who inherit their power.

ethnic: related to a group of people from a particular country or culture.

exile: the state of being sent away by force from a person's homeland.

ghettos: poor areas of a city where many people of a particular minority group live because of economic or social pressures.

minority group: a small number of people within a much larger society, who share characteristics that are different from most other people's.

moderate: not too extreme in any way.

Nativity: the birth of Jesus Christ.

navigable: able to be travelled on, especially by ship or boat.

patriots: people who are extremely loyal to their countries or homelands.

persecuted: treated cruelly because of background, beliefs or race.

reform: change that is intended to correct faults or make improvements.

religious tolerance: allowing the practice of all faiths and religions.

thatch: plant materials such as straw, reeds or palm leaves that are used as a covering to provide shelter.

vocational: related to an occupation, profession or skilled trade.

waterways: bodies of water, such as rivers and canals, used for travel.

More Books to Read

Auschwitz. Clive A. Lawton (Franklin Watts)

Auschwitz. Visiting the Past series. Jane Shuter (Heinemann Library)

The Changing Face Of: Poland. Barbara and Charles Everett (Hodder Wayland)

Communism. Ideas of the Modern World series. Nigel Richie (Hodder Wayland)

A Hero and the Holocaust: The Story of Janusz Korczak and His Children.
David A. Adler (Holiday House)

I Have Lived a Thousand Years. Livia Bitton-Jackson (Simon and Schuster)

The Story of the Holocaust. Clive A. Lawton (Franklin Watts)

Web Sites

www.artyzm.com/matejko/poczet/e_poczet.htm

www.auschwitz.org.pl/html/eng/start/index.php

www.poland.pl/info/information_ about_poland.htm

Due to the dynamic nature of the Internet, some web sites stay current longer than others. To find additional web sites, use a reliable search engine with one or more of the following keywords to help you locate information about Poland. Keywords: *Carpathian Mountains, Gdansk, KrakÛw, Vistula River, Lech Walesa.*

Note to parents and teachers
Every effort has been made by the Publishers to ensure that these web sites are suitable for children, that they are of the highest educational value, and that they contain no inappropriate or offensive material. However, because of the nature of the Internet, it is impossible to guarantee that the contents of these sites will not be altered. We strongly advise that Internet access is supervised by a responsible adult.

Index